Caster Semenya Biography Book

The Inspiring Story of a South African Middle Distance Runner

By Lisa Robert

Copyright © 2023 [Lisa Roberts]. All rights reserved.

This work is protected by copyright law and may not be reproduced, distributed, transmitted, displayed, published, or broadcast without the prior written permission of the copyright owner. You may not alter or remove any trademark, copyright, or other notice from copies of the content.

Unauthorized use and/or duplication of this material without express and written permission from the copyright owner is strictly prohibited. Excerpts and links may be used, provided that full and clear credit is given to [Lisa Roberts] with appropriate and specific direction to the original content.

TABLE OF CONTENTS

Copyright

TABLE OF CONTENTS

Introduction

CHAPTER ONE

  A Childhood in Limpopo

CHAPTER TWO

  Discovering a Talent

CHAPTER THREE

  Rising Through the Ranks

CHAPTER FOUR

The Olympic Dream

CHAPTER FIVE

Controversy and Triumph

CHAPTER SIX

The Unwavering Spirit

Introduction

In the world of middle-distance running, one name stands out not only for athletic prowess but also for daring, perseverance, and unrelenting drive that have defied the sport's standards and customs. Caster Semenya, a middle-distance runner from South Africa, has become a symbol of unbreakable power both on and off the track. This biography honors her astonishing journey, remarkable achievements, and unwavering spirit.

Caster Semenya was born in the Limpopo province of South Africa on January 7, 1991, in the community of Ga-Masehlong. Her narrative is a monument to the power of perseverance, beginning with her humble beginnings in this rural community, where the dusty paths of her childhood served as a canvas for her budding passion for running. Caster's journey is about more than just winning races; it's about breaking down barriers and reinventing the fundamental definition of competitiveness.

This biography will take you on an enthralling trip through her life, chapter by chapter. Caster's narrative is one of raw passion, determination, and a natural grace that would prophesy her exceptional destiny, from her early years in Ga-Masehlong, where the simplicity of rural life encouraged her love of running, to her rapid rise on the global stage of middle-distance running.

We will look at the life of a young girl who, despite all odds, chased her aspirations with unwavering tenacity. Her journey was not without difficulties. Her physical education instructor, who saw her outstanding potential, first noticed her during her early years in high school. Caster's talent quickly propelled her to the national and international stage, and her name became synonymous with athletics.

Caster Semenya's road, however, was far from smooth. Her meteoric rise is closely related to a controversy that drew international notice and sparked debates about gender and identity in sports. As she emerged as a strong force on the track, she was surrounded by questions and scrutiny, throwing a spotlight on her identity as a woman in a sport that frequently grapples with gender ambiguities.

The Beijing Olympics in 2008 were a watershed moment in her career. Caster Semenya battled the world's best middle-distance runners there and etched her mark in history. Her victory, coupled by controversy and arguments regarding her gender, elevated her to the status of a figure of tenacity and defiance. She not only defeated her competition, but also the obstacles that threatened to wreck her career.

This biography dives into the issues, legal fights, and widespread popular support that characterized Caster Semenya's path. It reveals a woman's indomitable spirit who, rather of surrendering to external demands, chose to be herself and continue to run her race, both on and off the track.

However, Caster's narrative is more than just the difficulties and tribulations of an outstanding athlete.

It's also a story of empowerment, motivation, and activism. It's the story of a lady who utilized her platform to bring attention to concerns beyond athletics. Her bravery has made her a role model for the LGBTQ+ community, athletes, and gender equality campaigners.

Throughout these pages, you will also learn about the person behind the runner—Caster Semenya's personal and private life. You'll learn about her relationships, her philanthropic efforts, and her unrelenting dedication to make the world a better place.

Caster Semenya's legacy extends beyond her extraordinary physical achievements to her influence on the world of sports, her motivation to future athletes, and her challenge to established standards in her pursuit of gender equality in sports.

Prepare to be inspired and affected by a story that goes far beyond the finish line as you embark on this trip through Caster Semenya's life. It's the story of a South African middle-distance runner who overcame the odds, pushed the boundaries, and paved the way for a more inclusive and equal world. This biography honors her extraordinary journey and welcomes you to be a part of Caster Semenya: The South African Middle Distance Runner's inspiring story.

CHAPTER ONE

A Childhood in Limpopo

Caster Semenya's path to become a great middle-distance runner began in the lovely community of Ga-Masehlong, which is located in South Africa's Limpopo region. Caster was the third of five siblings born on January 7, 1991, in the Semenya family, and her parents, Jacob and Dorcus Semenya, were hardworking folks dedicated to providing for their children. The Semenya home was full of love and support, with a strong emphasis on education and morals.

Life in Ga-Masehlong was characterized by simplicity and strong community relationships. The community was known for its communal character, with neighbors who were more than just friends but extended family. Caster developed a strong feeling of camaraderie, solidarity, and perseverance as a result of his experiences in this environment.

Caster had his early schooling in Ga-Masehlong's public schools. Her instructors and peers began to notice something unique about her during these formative years. She demonstrated a great work ethic and determination in all of her endeavors, whether academic or athletic. Her teachers praised her attention to her studies, and her students admired her persistent dedication.

Caster Semenya's incredible athletic path began with a succession of exciting moments that revealed her natural potential. She had exceptional speed and endurance from an early age, which set her apart from her colleagues.

Caster's inherent athletic prowess shone strongly in Ga-Masehlong's dusty fields and rocky terrain. She'd effortlessly race alongside her buddies, astounded by her speed and agility. Caster's love of running was a profound passion etched into her heart, not just a competitive desire.

One of her earliest memories was of sprinting across the fields barefoot with a resolve that belied her age. Her parents realized her potential after witnessing her innate talent. Jacob and Dorcus Semenya pushed their daughter to pursue her athletic abilities, recognizing that her talent was a special gift that needed to be nurtured.

Caster began running competitively in the local elementary school in Ga-Masehlong, where she joined the school's athletics squad. Her coaches quickly recognized her as a tremendous talent, citing her incredible speed and endurance. Her several successes made her a well-known personality in her school and village.

Caster's reputation as a gifted runner gradually spread beyond the bounds of Ga-Masehlong as she continued to compete in local races and tournaments. Her commitment, unwavering training, and unyielding spirit fuelled her pursuit of excellence. Her talent was evident, and her list of accomplishments grew, indicating a bright future in athletics. Caster Semenya's upbringing in Ga-Masehlong, as well as her undeniable athletic talent, laid the groundwork for an astonishing journey that would lead her to become one of the world's most recognized middle-distance runners. Her narrative is not just one of personal victory, but also one of the strength, determination, and everlasting support of her family and community.

The simplicity of her early years in Ga-Masehlong, combined with her inherent athletic ability, would serve as the foundation for her future success. Nobody could have predicted that this ambitious young South African rural girl would go on to inspire the world with her outstanding talent and unshakeable passion.

CHAPTER TWO

Discovering a Talent

Caster Semenya's extraordinary career as a middle-distance runner began in the heart of Ga-Masehlong, a little community located in South Africa's Limpopo region. Her extraordinary potential was first identified and nurtured by her committed physical education (PE) instructor, who was instrumental in molding the course of her life.

Caster, like her friends in the hamlet, was an enthusiastic and vivacious child as she grew up. Her PE teacher, Samuel Sepeng, however, noticed something truly unique in her. Mr. Sepeng, a sports enthusiast with a good eye for talent, saw in young Caster the raw potential to become an exceptional athlete.

Her teacher's continuous support and advice defined Caster's formative years. He pushed her to participate in a variety of activities, but it was on the athletics track that her exceptional talent began to shine. Under Mr. Sepeng's attentive eye, she displayed exceptional speed, endurance, and a natural aptitude for running that distinguished her from her colleagues.

Mr. Sepeng, understanding Caster's potential for greatness, became her coach and champion. He worked relentlessly to give her the resources and chances she needed to develop her gift. He was her coach on many occasions, fine-tuning her techniques and ensuring she had access to the greatest training available in their limited, village-based facilities.

Caster Semenya's friendship with her PE teacher extended beyond athletics. It was a collaboration that went beyond the track. Mr. Sepeng instilled in her the principles of tenacity, discipline, and dedication, which she would need to succeed as a world-class athlete. His guidance was crucial in helping Caster understand the value of hard work and striving for perfection.

Caster entered her first competitive races while she continued to practice with Mr. Sepeng. It wasn't long before her outstanding talent was recognized by a larger audience. She frequently surpassed her rivals in local track and field events, leaving spectators in amazement of her speed and determination.

Her success on the local circuit quickly led to invitations to regional and national championships.

She won her first important triumphs during these early years of her career. Caster Semenya didn't just win races; she dominated them. Her performances in a variety of middle-distance events, particularly the 800 meters, drew widespread attention and acclaim in South Africa.

Her first national title was a key milestone in her career, kicking off a journey that would lead her to the international scene. Caster's self-confidence and belief in her ability grew stronger with each victory. She wasn't just competing; she was setting new benchmarks for women's middle-distance running.

Caster's early triumphs were a testament to her innate talent as well as the time and effort she put into her training. Her extraordinary accomplishments were a source of pride for her family, village, and mentor, Mr. Sepeng. They had beaten the odds by nurturing a talent that would eventually capture the globe.

These early challenges and achievements lay the groundwork for a remarkable sports career. Caster Semenya's journey from a modest Limpopo town to becoming a global athletics sensation was just getting started. Her gift, nurtured by her dedicated PE teacher and undeniable success in her initial competitions, would soon propel her to new heights, laying the groundwork for a story of resilience, tenacity, and inspiration that would inspire future generations.

CHAPTER THREE

Rising Through the Ranks

Caster Semenya's journey to greatness began long before she became a worldwide star on the track. Her outstanding aptitude as a middle-distance runner originally emerged during her high school years in Limpopo, South Africa.

Caster Semenya's high school years were essential in her growth as an athlete. She quickly gained notoriety for her extraordinary athletic abilities while attending Nthema Secondary School in her hometown of Ga-Masehlong. Her school provided as an important breeding ground for her skill, and it was here that she first began to shine on the track.

One of her first major achievements came in 2008, when she competed in the South African Junior Championships. Caster dominated the competition, winning gold in the 800 meters. This not only demonstrated her quickness, but also her incredible endurance. Her high school coaches were crucial in mentoring her and identifying her potential, providing the necessary support and training to develop her into the accomplished athlete she is today.

Caster Semenya's amazing achievements in high school did not go unnoticed by the national and international athletics communities. Her meteoric rise in South African athletics created the way for her to represent her country on the international level.

She accomplished the incredible achievement of qualifying for the South African Olympic team at the age of 17 in 2008. Her qualification for the Beijing Olympics demonstrated her exceptional talent and ability to compete at the highest levels of the sport.

South Africa had discovered a budding star, and Caster's trip to the Olympics demonstrated her determination and amazing ability.

Her appearance at the 2008 Beijing Olympics was a watershed moment in her career. She won the gold medal in the women's 800 meters after a spectacular performance against the world's best runners. Caster Semenya crossed the finish line in amazement, setting a new national record and declaring her entrance as a strong presence in middle-distance running. Her victory was not only a personal triumph, but also a watershed moment for South Africa and African sports.

International recognition followed quickly. Caster's astounding accomplishments and evident talent catapulted her into the international spotlight. She became a symbol of inspiration for young athletes across the African continent, demonstrating that ambitions can be realized through hard work and dedication. Her accomplishment paved the path for more diversity and representation in middle-distance running.

Aside from the medals and records, Caster's international prominence spoke to her character and resilience. She faced attention and controversy because of her gender, but she persisted in her pursuit of excellence. Her courage to overcome misfortune and survive on her own terms inspired numerous others throughout the world.

Caster Semenya's rise from Limpopo's high school tracks to international acclaim is a monument to her tremendous talent, devotion, and unbreakable spirit. Her high school accomplishments lay the framework for a career that not only altered middle-distance running but also challenged gender and fitness stereotypes. Caster's rise up the ranks is a story of unshakable dedication and the enduring ability of athletics to break down boundaries and inspire future generations.

Her high school achievements, combined with national and international acclaim, laid the groundwork for an outstanding athletic career that continues to touch and influence the sports world. Caster Semenya's legacy goes beyond records and victories; it is a monument to the human spirit's perseverance and ability to overcome obstacles and limits.

CHAPTER FOUR

The Olympic Dream

Caster Semenya's route to the Olympics in Beijing was marked by unyielding devotion and meticulous preparation. As she began her journey toward fulfilling her Olympic dream, it became clear that her inherent talent, tenacity, and the unwavering support of her coach and family were the foundations of her success.

Semenya, like other athletes, faced significant physical and emotional hurdles in the run-up to the Beijing Olympics. Her training schedule was rigorous, requiring numerous hours of practice and conditioning. She pushed herself to the breaking point, perfecting her technique and increasing her physical endurance.

Her coach, who noticed her exceptional talent and worked tirelessly to maximize her potential, was a defining characteristic that set her apart. Their collaboration was founded on trust, mutual goals, and a thorough grasp of Semenya's special qualities. The coach not only assisted her in improving her running technique, but also in dealing with the pressure and expectations that come with competing on the world's biggest stage.

Semenya's excitement and nervousness were obvious as the Beijing Olympics approached. She represented her family, her coach, and her country, in addition to herself. Her drive to achieve was strengthened by the weight of that obligation. Her daily routine included not only physical but also mental preparation. She sharpened her focus, built mental fortitude, and pictured success on the track.

Semenya arrived in Beijing as one of South Africa's most promising athletes, thanks to her undeniable skill, unwavering work ethic, and strong support system. Her incredible road to the Olympics was not without its hardships, but the difficulties only served to reinforce her drive.

Caster Semenya made her international debut at the Beijing Olympics. She was set to fight against the world's best middle-distance runners, a difficult field of opponents who had also dedicated their life to achieving their Olympic goals.

The atmosphere in Beijing was intense, with all eyes on the athletes competing in the middle-distance events. Semenya's competitors were similarly motivated, each with their own set of strengths and techniques. Some were seasoned veterans, while others were budding talents, all aiming for Olympic gold.

The 800-meter race was extremely contested, with Semenya competing against formidable opponents who had established themselves on many international platforms. The stakes were high, and the entire world was watching. Despite this, it was the circumstances that brought out the best in her.

Tension loomed heavily in the air on the day of the 800-meter final. Semenya, the youthful South African sensation, competed against competitors from all over the world. The race began with the firing of the starting gun. She charged forward with a tenacity that astounded the onlookers. Her innate speed and flawless form catapulted her ahead, putting her neck and neck with the greatest in the world.

During the race's final stretch, it became clear that Semenya's talent and commitment were unrivaled. She pushed ahead at breakneck pace, leaving her competitors in her wake. The stadium exploded in applause as she crossed the finish line. Caster Semenya had not only won the gold medal, but had done so with authority, crossing the finish line with a happy smile.

The triumph attested to her unwavering dedication as well as the steadfast support of her coach, family, and country. Caster Semenya, a young South African woman, had prevailed against the world's greatest middle-distance runners, achieving her Olympic goal and engraving her name in the annals of athletic excellence.

The Olympics in Beijing were a watershed moment in Caster Semenya's career. It was a moment that demonstrated her extraordinary talent, unbreakable character, and ability to rise to the situation while fighting against the best in the world. This triumph marked the start of a remarkable journey in which she would continue to inspire and leave a lasting impact on the worlds of sports and gender equality.

CHAPTER FIVE

Controversy and Triumph

Caster Semenya's route to Olympic gold was marred by a one-of-a-kind and difficult stumbling block: the gender debate that pushed her into the global spotlight. Caster, who was born in the small Limpopo community of Ga-Masehlong, showed early promise in middle-distance running. Rumors and guesses about her gender began to circulate as she began to make her imprint on the track.

The International Association of Athletics Federations (IAAF) began gender verification testing, putting Semenya under investigation and raising questions about her identity. The scandal sparked a frenzy of media coverage and public debate. This experience was both professionally and personally taxing. Semenya found herself at the center of a controversy about gender equality and sports justice. The entire world watched as she endured through this trying time, demonstrating tenacity and strength in the face of adversity.

The 2009 World Championships in Berlin were the zenith of Caster Semenya's athletic career. She won the gold medal in the 800 meters with a dominant performance, demonstrating her middle-distance running prowess. This victory should have been a triumphant celebration of her exceptional talent and hard effort. It was, however, overshadowed by the gender issue that had raged since the exams began.

The debate resurfaced following Semenya's gold medal win at the World Championships. Her athletic dominance fueled speculation about perceived biological advantages she might have. While the debate raged on, Semenya remained unwavering in her dedication to running and ambition to compete on the world stage.

As the globe dealt with the issues of gender and athletics, some questioned Semenya's athletic feats, while others embraced her victories. She kept pushing herself, achieving records and receiving honors, but the controversy followed her every step of the way.

Caster Semenya demonstrated amazing grace under pressure throughout the gender debate and her Olympic gold medal victory. She never let the issue define or discourage her from following her aspirations. Semenya's journey exemplifies unshakable dedication, tenacity in the face of adversity, and courage in asserting one's identity.

Caster Semenya's legacy stretches beyond the track as the debate over gender and sports continues. Her narrative has sparked debate regarding the acceptance and equitable treatment of all athletes, regardless of gender identity. Her steadfast attitude in the face of tragedy has inspired numerous people throughout the world, serving as a light of hope for those who have encountered discrimination, intolerance, or miscommunication.

Caster Semenya's impact on the world of athletics is defined by more than just medals and records. It demonstrates her bravery and determination in the face of hardship. Her narrative inspires society to reconsider and redefine the limits of justice and diversity in sports.

While the gender debate and its attendant problems were unquestionably unpleasant, they constituted a watershed moment in Caster Semenya's life. Her victories and dedication to the sport of middle-distance running have left an everlasting imprint, one that advocates for a more equal and inclusive future for all athletes. Her legacy is more than just gold medals; it is about battling for identity and justice on and off the track.

CHAPTER SIX

The Unwavering Spirit

Caster Semenya's steadfast dedication and unbreakable personality shone brilliantly amid the gender issue and legal fights that raged around her career. She was undeterred by the difficulties she encountered and continued to pursue her passion for middle-distance running. This chapter delves into her victorious return to the track and her incredible path to the 2016 Olympics in Rio de Janeiro.

Caster Semenya found herself at a crossroads when the tempest of gender tests and legal wrangling calmed. Many people were dejected or discouraged, but Semenya's spirit was unbroken. She knew she had a talent and a great love for running, and she was determined to show it on the track.

The sports world and her admirers awaited Semenya's comeback to competitive racing with bated breath. The entire world was watching to see if she could keep up the remarkable form that had distinguished her early career. Her persistent focus and rigorous preparation demonstrated her determination to silence the critics and reaffirm her standing as a world-class athlete.

Caster Semenya's tenacity shone through during her return campaign. She used her suffering as fuel for her fire, changing it into an unwavering resolve to succeed. Her unshakeable spirit was going to be revealed to the rest of the world.

Caster Semenya went on the voyage to the 2016 Rio Olympics carrying not just the hopes and dreams of her South African compatriots, but also numerous admirers from around the world. This was more than just an Olympic quest; it was a journey of atonement and empowerment.

Semenya's journey to Rio was distinguished by rigorous training, harsh competition, and unrelenting dedication to her objective. She understood she wasn't just running for herself, but for everyone who had stood by her in the face of adversity. The strain was intense, but her commitment remained unwavering.

The 800m event at Rio de Janeiro was a watershed point in Semenya's career. It was her chance to shine on the international scene and prove that she was back and stronger than ever. Her steely resolve and the enthusiasm of an athlete who had experienced the most difficult of journeys were obvious as she stepped onto the track for the final.

Caster Semenya won the 800 meters race in the Rio Olympics in a performance that will be remembered for years to come. Her victory was more than just a gold medal; it was a triumph of spirit and a declaration of her status as an elite middle-distance runner. The world witnessed an extraordinary athlete who faced hardship head on, conquered it, and emerged as a champion.

Semenya's road to Rio was a redemption story, an inspiring story of resilience and unrelenting commitment. Her Olympic win in 2016 was about more than simply medals and records; it was about breaking down barriers and smashing preconceived preconceptions. It delivered a strong message that, no matter what obstacles were in the way, the spirit of a real athlete could overcome them.

Caster Semenya's return to the track and her road to the Rio Olympics demonstrate her tenacity. They highlight her triumph over adversity through fortitude, determination, and an unrelenting dedication to her passion for middle-distance running. Her tale encourages not only athletes, but all people to face adversity with unflinching determination and to pursue their dreams regardless of the odds. Caster Semenya's journey to Rio is proof of the enduring power of the human spirit.

Printed in Great Britain
by Amazon